The Dogs' Guide To Humans

Written by Susan Griffiths

Illustrated by Kelvin Hucker

Contents	Page
Chapter 1. *Dogs in charge!*	4
Chapter 2. *The head and neck*	8
Chapter 3. *The arms and hands*	13
Chapter 4. *The legs and feet*	18
Chapter 5. *The chest, stomach, and skin*	23
Chapter 6. *Choosing human puppies*	29
Verse	32

Rigby

The Dogs' Guide To Humans

With these characters ...

Professor
Wolf Mutt

One Human

"Give this book

In this new book, for dogs only, you'll learn how to choose, train, and play with a human pet. But don't let any humans read this book! If they do, we will be in big trouble!

back to the nearest dog!"

Chapter 1.

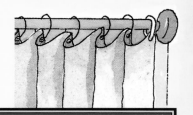

WARNING

This secret guide is for dogs only.
It must not be read by humans, or it might
explode! If you are a human, give this book
back to the nearest dog!

Okay, now that
we've scared off any
human readers,
let's begin. Welcome
to *The Dogs' Guide
To Humans*.
My name is
Professor Wolf Mutt.
I will teach you the
facts about people.

A Human

In this book, you will learn how a human body is perfectly made to help us. You will learn how to train your human to do everything you want.

But remember: humans must never learn that we are in charge of the world. If they find out, they will not be happy. Unhappy humans are no fun!

When I started studying humans, I found out they were poorly made for life in a dog's world.

They have no tail to wag, not much fur, and a poor sense of smell.

Humans are lucky that we have chosen to help them. Without us, they would have nothing to do. Luckily, we have given humans a purpose — a purpose they have a perfect body for!

In the next five chapters, I'll show you how the human body is useful to dogs.

So, before you start reading, make sure there are no humans nearby!

Look around! Sniff the air! Listen carefully! If it's safe, start reading the next chapter!

Chapter 2.

The Head

A human's head is at the top of its body, not at the front. This means that they miss out on seeing lots of interesting things in the grass.

Humans also find it hard to eat off the floor. This is why they have to sit on chairs and eat from tables.

So, what is good about a human's head?

Humans can see meat and bones in a butcher's shop much better than we can!

Humans have ears and noses, but not as good as ours. Human noses can't even smell cats! Their ears are so bad that they need us to listen for visitors arriving. Humans rely on us more than they know.

Like dogs, humans have mouths in their heads, too. Just for fun, humans can be trained to whistle when we run toward them! This makes them feel important.

The Neck

Inside a human's neck is a voice box. Their voice box only makes quiet barks.

Humans are not very smart, as they can't understand us. With a little practice, we can *easily* understand what humans are barking about.

Some human barks are:

1. "Do you want some food?"
2. "Do you want to go for a walk?"
3. "Do you want to play?"
4. "Do you want a bath?"

You should train your human to say the first three barks by wagging your tail. When you hear the fourth bark, run away and hide.

Other barks we don't like to hear are:

"Stay!"
"Outside!"
"Sit!"

Ignore those barks. Humans don't like being ignored. They soon learn not to bother making these barks.

Remember: it's important that you never let a human know that you can understand everything they say.

Chapter 3.

The Arms

A human's front legs are called arms. They are useless for walking on, but they are useful for other purposes.

Humans can be trained to use their arms for throwing balls and sticks for us to chase. Arms are also useful for opening refrigerator doors.

At the lower end of their arms are wrists. Wrists are useful for keeping watches on. Watches help humans know when to do jobs for us. Jobs that humans need to do on time for us are:

- morning walk
- feeding us breakfast
- reminding us to nap
- feeding us lunch
- feeding us dinner
- ball throwing

Without watches, humans might forget about us and leave us at home alone. This would be terrible, as we may fall asleep in front of the TV. Humans must be trained to do *all* their jobs *every* day, on time.

The Hands

The most useful part of a human's body is their hands. Hands are really just large front paws. Their long bony ends are called fingers and thumbs.

With fingers and thumbs, humans can pick up things like food bowls without using their teeth! They can even use tools like can openers. Amazing!

At the end of their fingers and
thumbs are short claws called
fingernails. Fingernails are good
for scratching our hard-to-reach
itches. That feels *really* good!

Hands are useful for holding our leashes. Sometimes, we will let humans feed us small pieces of food from their hands.

Never, ever, do any jobs for a human. If they know we can do many of the jobs ourselves, they will make us do all the work!

Chapter 4.

The Legs

Humans use their back legs to walk around on. They would have much more fun if they walked on all fours — but we are happy that they don't. Their arms, or front legs, are kept free to play with us and feed us.

Legs are good for moving humans to fun places, like parks. In parks, humans should be trained to move their legs quicker. Then they can fetch our balls and sticks for us quickly.

Near the bottom of a human's legs are ankles. Ankles are easy to bite, if a human does something we don't like. Once a human is bitten on the ankle, he or she usually behaves better.

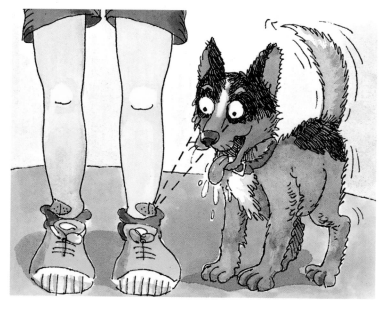

Never bite a human unless you tell them what they should stop doing. Usually a growl will stop most humans from doing anything bad. If they still behave badly — take a little nibble!

The Feet

At the end of the legs is another pair of paws called feet. People put socks and shoes on their feet. These are great to chew on. Remember to chew on socks and shoes *after* a human has worn them. They will smell and taste much better!

For fun, you can hide a sock and a shoe. You can amuse yourself for hours by following your human around as they look for them. Remember to look innocent and wag your tail.

Then, pretend to sniff out the hidden sock and shoe, and you will get a treat. Most humans are so silly they don't even know we're teasing them!

Chapter 5.

The Chest and Stomach

Between a human's arms is their chest and stomach. They are perfect parts of the body to jump on, stretch out on, and scratch on.

When humans wear clothes, these parts are extra soft and warm— perfect for snoozing on, too!

Never let a human sleep on your bed. If they find out how comfortable dog beds are, there won't be any space left for you! They might also snore and keep you awake all night!

Like dogs, humans can eat meat and vegetables. We try to eat as much of the humans' food as we can. We are lucky they don't know how delicious our dog food and smelly bones are!

The Skin

Human skin has very little fur on it. They have to wear furry things, called clothes, to keep warm.

Clothes are fun because people hang them out to dry on a clothesline. Now, we can play the *best* game!
The aim of the game is to jump up and pull all the clothes to the ground *before* the human sees you.

Socks are worth one point, T-shirts are worth three points, and shirts are worth five.

Clothes are useful because they have pockets. Pockets are perfect for holding balls and dog treats. This means a human is always ready to play with us or give us a treat.

Once the human has picked up all the clothes off the ground, they will put them into a clothes basket. You *must* lie on the clothes! Your hair and smell will cover their clothes. Now other dogs will know that your human is already owned by a dog — you!

Chapter 6.

Congratulations! Now that you have learned about humans, you are ready to choose your very own human pet!

Humans come in all shapes, sizes, and colors. Choose human puppies, called children. There are two types: boys and girls. They are easy to train, happy to play for hours, and like to take care of us.

So, what should you look for when you choose a boy or a girl?

Choose a child who smiles a lot.
This human pet will always
be happy to see you.

Choose a child with plenty
of energy. He or she will play
with you more than a lazy human.

Choose a child that doesn't like eating
their dinner. This means there will be
plenty of leftover food for you to eat.

Most of all, choose a child who *thinks*
he or she is smarter than you. That
way, they will never know that *you* are
the smartest dog. You'll get your own
way all of the time!

But remember: *never* let your human see a copy of this book! If they find out how smart we really are, there will be a worldwide dog disaster!

Listen! What's that? It sounds like footsteps! Quick, hide this book. Wag your tail and roll over. Look as cute as you can. Those silly humans will never suspect a thing!

"A Dog's World"

Human bodies are quite useless,
They really don't work well,
Poor eyes, poor ears, no paws, no tail,
And a hopeless sense of smell.

It's lucky for them that we're around
To keep them out of strife,
Without us dogs, they'd quickly lose
A purpose for their life!

Let humans all remember,
Even though they are quite large,
That it's a DOG'S world they live in,
And the dogs are all in charge!